Palmettos & Pluff Mud

TALES OF A LOST LOWCOUNTRY LIFE

ALSO BY GUILDS HOLLOWELL

Signature Tastes of Charleston

Signature Sips: Anthology of Charleston's Cocktails

ALSO BY STEVEN W. SILER

Signature Tastes series of cookbooks

Hardtack & Haversacks

Playing With Fires

TIDELANDS

"...for those whose lives are pulled by the tides."

an imprint of

12 SIRENS PUBLISHING CO.

GUILDS HOLLOWELL
with
STEVEN W. SILER

Palmettos & Pluff Mud

TALES OF A LOST LOWCOUNTRY LIFE

Like all books that are culled from memories, this one recalls the adventures of the author, from his perspective. Any offense, revealing of dark family secrets or resemblance to persons, living or dead, is purely coincidental.

PUBLISHED BY TIDELANDS
AN IMPRINT OF 12 SIRENS, LLC
334 East Bay Street, Charleston, South Carolina 29401

TIDELANDS IS A TRADEMARK OF 12 SIRENS, LLC

Endpaper photograph: From the Charleston Historical Society

Book design by Steven W. Siler

Library of Congress Cataloging-in-Publication Data
Hollowell, Guilds Hollowell.
Palmettos & Pluff Mud/ Guilds Hollowell.-1st ed.
p. cm.
1. Hollowell, Guilds- South Carolina living. 2. Coastal-South
3. Nature-Essays.

ISBN: 978-1-927458-31-0

PRINTING IN THE UNITED STATES OF AMERICA

December 2017

First Edition

1 3 5 7 9 10 8 6 4 2

This book is dedicated to
Caddie,
who by being my true North,
pointed me to my true South

CONTENTS

INTRODUCTION

"My wound is geography. It is also my anchorage, my port of call."

Pat Conroy, Prince of Tides

So begins a soliloquy that tells a fictional story rooted in a Lowcountry reality. For many of us here, these words hearken to a simpler time, either from our own childhood or one that we wish we had enjoyed. For Guilds Hollowell, the Lowcountry has proved to be not only an anchorage, but in some ways the siren call, a thin quiet song teasing his ears after four decades in foreign (read: "furrin'" or also known as, not from Here) lands. It's a bittersweet tune, like all good and great love affairs, and for us, the beginning is remembered as the sweetest time.

I have had the pleasure of Guilds' friendship from the moment we first encountered each other overlooking the Ashley River at an all-too-common "food and wine" event in Charleston. I recognized a kindred soul, which might not speak well for either of us. Taking a food tour with him later, learning about my home city (which I swore I knew all about, and was thankfully mistaken), his gift of simple storytelling was on display, along with something else... a love and longing for a nearer past that was unmistakably clear.

I heard two of the following stories in an audio recording of Guilds recounting them. The lilt, the cadence and utter lack of an accent (Remember, we are Southerners. We don't have accents because God talks like we do...) had me shaking my head in cringing recognition and pangs of nostalgia. He did not have a choice in writing these down; he had an anthropological duty to do it. These are remembrances that stand as endangered mile markers of our sojourn in the city of Charleston. In short, we live and prosper in a city literally built on history, and yet we have to defend our own nostalgia from the ravages of progress.

So, grab a cool one from the icebox and read on. When the grind on the Mark Clark or the Crosstown or even Maybank has you twisted up, take a swig of both of these. And like that first sip or first kiss, I imagine you will find them as refreshing and restorative as they were when first enjoyed.

Steven W. Siler
Old Village, Mount Pleasant, South Carolina, USA

Foreword

Jack Hitt, the best-selling author of Off the Road, which was made into the movie ***The Way****, with Martin Sheen. He is also a Charleston native. Additionally, Jack is a contributing editor to Harper's, The New York Times Magazine, and This American Life, as well as being a childhood friend and classmate of Guilds.*

Growing up in Charleston, my friends and I liked to play outside, relying upon the simple things we had at hand. Like tourists, for instance. They can be found scattered all over Charleston—wandering on foot with far-off gazes, reading those little plaques bolted on every house, or gathering in pods at a garden gate to glimpse the depravity of azaleas. Giving a tourist the run-around was a traditional sport for Charlestonians, and one enjoyed by locals of every age and acquaintance. We were all in on the deal.

During my teenage years, the mid 70s, the carriage tour trade took off. Several friends of mine won the plum spot of donning a sash and driving a sweet-tempered nag up and down our streets while reciting a story line whose bluster sounded very much like actual history.

One of my childhood friends drove the carriage back then and the way one game worked was this: If he was ambling down Meeting Street in his tourist-crammed surrey, he might catch my eye as I walked by, and his narration would suddenly switch out to the swashbuckling tale of the only female general of the Confederacy: "Jacquiline Hitt, and she lived and died"—and then he would point—"in that very house"—whatever house was just behind me. His awesome tale would unfold with increasingly preposterous but deadpan detail. The game was to keep a straight face as I raised one arm, like a helpful game-show hostess in lamé, to indicate the window through which General Jacquie met her God. The payoff was the papparazzi-like explosion of a dozen Kodak cameras clicking away.

In those days, ***Gone With the Wind*** was still a seasonal TV indulgence and, even though the movie is unbearable, Charlestonians love to isolate one little moment. Just before Rhett utters the classic line,

"Frankly my dear, I don't give a damn," Scarlett asks him where is he going to go, and Rhett says he's going home to Charleston—to see if "there isn't something left in life of charm and grace." It was always a surprise to us kids just how many tourists remembered that line and would ask if we knew "where Rhett Butler was buried."

Of course we knew—because when it came to shining on tourists, we were more ruthless than Incan warriors dispatching conquistadors over fatal mountain ridges to El Dorado. "Oh, sure, Rhett Butler's grave, just up here—he's buried in St. Philip's graveyard, just inside the gate—can't miss it."

Punking folks from off was always fun, but it wasn't really why we did it. The real point was to have a story to tell somewhere down the line, later that day. If somebody were to ask, how's it going and all you had to say was, well, pretty good, you sounded like a retiree or somebody from the upstate. People say Charlestonians talk funny, by which they typically mean the intercoastal dialects, but they also mean that folks in the low country don't really speak words or even sentences. The local vernacular is built out of full-blown stories.

In the past, a few brave locals have tried to put on paper some of these stories, both true and not-so-much: Debose Heyward, Josephine Pinckney, Pat Conroy, Josephine Humphreys. Now comes Guilds to capture a few of them from a different generation. Leafing through these, some of which I tell myself, I only wish that he had numbered them. That would save a lot of time, on all kinds of occasions. For a local, a brisk ten minute walk to a corner store can take a full hour because he might have to say good morning to somebody he hadn't seen in a while, and then listen while the other person says good morning back. And if somebody else wanders up, well, then everybody's late for lunch.

Jack Hitt

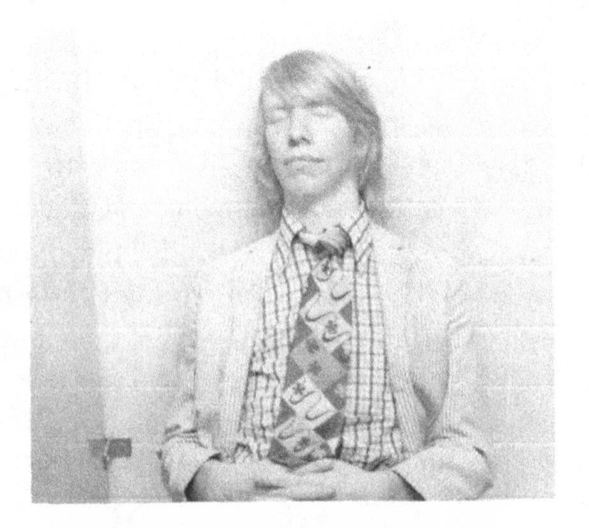

Jack Hitt, dreaming of future days

Captain Holz

Porter-Gaud School is an icon of Charleston's educational institutions. It was established from a combination of three different academies:, the Porter Military Academy (founded immediately after the War Between the States to educate homeless and orphaned children), the Gaud School for Boys and the Watt School. The school has been historically associated with the Episcopal church, and consequently its biggest rival is its Catholic counterpart in college preparatory education, Bishop England High School. Go Cyclones!

Back in the day, I attended Porter Gaud School, which was at the time an all-boys school. Since some of it's roots originated from Porter Military Academy, all of my teachers were male, many of them former military: Major

Alexander, Colonel Freeman, Admiral Florence and Captain Holz for example. The one who sticks out in my mind is Cap'n Holz.

I remember meeting him for the first time. It would have been in 9th or 10th grade, whatever year you are forced to take Algebra and Trigonometry. I walked into the classroom and sat right in the front row (arguably not the smartest decision I have made). Captain Holz walked into the classroom with his satchel and stick...he always carried this large leather satchel and a big stick, like a ¾" dowel. He would put the satchel on the trashcan next to his desk and then slap the satchel with the stick to call the class to order. The first time he slapped it, it scared the hell out of me. He then looked at me and said, "Hollowell, I've heard about you. You think you're going to pass this course?"

I popped off, “Yes sir!”.

“You wanna make a bet?”, he said ominously.

Thus began the lessons, of both math and life.

The way he taught was cool. Once he slapped down that satchel, he would ask if there were any questions about the previous night’s assignment. If not, he would just move on to the next assignment by saying “Turn to page...”. He was not your typical teacher: he figured if you didn’t have any questions, there was nothing to discuss and you must know everything. You could take a nap, do English homework, whatever you wanted. Now if you had any questions, the man softened up. He would spend whatever time you needed to help you to understand the problem. But by God, you had better speak up when he asked!

His exams were interesting, consisting of only two or three questions. Consequently, your score was either a 100, 50 or 0, or if three questions a 100, 66, 33 or 0...hence the life lessons. Now this is back when we used slide rules and logarithmic tables and the such. One small error on reading a number on the chart was the difference between a perfect score and a perfect failure. It was hard, but it taught you to be detail-oriented, and to get it right the first time!

Understand, in a previous life, Captain Holz had been a navigator on a submarine. In the Navy, only the best sailors get to serve on a submarine...the most disciplined, the most exacting. I would watch some of the scholars in our class cry when he graded their papers as they handed them in. Since there were only 2 or 3 questions, he could grade it in a matter of seconds. Sometimes, someone might make a mental mistake like 2 x 3 = 5, or other such brain freezes. I remember one time when my friend David earned a rapid-fire 66. He protested, "Cap'n Holz, don't we get any partial credit?"

Cap'n Holz levelly replied, "You think they'd give me partial credit for *almost* making it to the North Pole?".

This is how I learned discipline under Cap'n Holz.

And he wasn't alone. Many of the teachers at Porter Gaud were amazing. Mr. Frampton was the Chemistry and Physics teacher. As happened often in the South, in the 1940's he actually taught my Dad at Moultrie High School in Mt. Pleasant. Again, the lessons were not just academic (mostly forgotten) but about getting through life (mostly remembered).

The teacher that helped me the most would have to be Ben Hutto. I sang in the first choir at Porter Gaud and throughout all my time there, under Mr. Hutto's tutelage. As often happens with impressionable teenagers, music struck a chord (pun intended) with me. Mr. Hutto helped to foster this love, and to structure my discipline to grow with it. Performing professionally today with my name on several albums, music has become a huge part of my life.

Thank you, Mr. Hutto. Looking back, my high school teachers are the most memorable of my life; they taught me to believe in myself.

Porter Military Academy, that would become
the Porter-Gaud school

66 Guilds Hollowell

Playing guitar

Turtle Eggs

The city of Charleston is protected by a series of barrier islands: Isle of Palms and Sullivan's to the north and James and John's Islands to the south. All four of these islands serve as nesting homes for the loggerhead and leatherback turtles. The females lay their eggs in nests along a line where the dunes meet the beach. In the early summer, the turtles hatch and make their way to the waterline to swim off to parts known and unknown.

My wife, Caddie, told me the other day that the Aquarium was releasing loggerhead turtles back into the wild. The Charleston Aquarium does such a fantastic job of not just educating the public about the incredible diversity of marine wildlife, but taking an active role in conservation in the city. Many a wounded turtle has been brought there for rehabilitation, and many a school child has delighted in a stingray tickling their open palms in search of a tasty morsel. I love everything they do.

That being said, I am reminded of a time when I was 5 or 6 years old. My parents would take me to the Isle of Palms and we would gather turtle eggs. Of course, this was a much different time. Nowadays it is illegal. Back then, we were just getting something to eat!

The first full moon in June, the loggerhead turtles would come out of the ocean and up on the beach. Using their flippers, they would drag themselves on shore and up close to the dunes, dig a hole and start to lay the eggs. After they had rested (laying a hundred or so eggs on land is tiring work for a critter used to the water!), they would then cover up the hole and begin their slow march back to the ocean surf.

Watching from a distance away on the beach, we would mark the locations of the nest and wait for them to leave. I suspect we knew it would be "impolite" to take the eggs with them watching us! Once the coast was clear, eager hands would dig up the sand like looking for so many white Easter eggs.

Once home, Mama would get the water pot going while we cleaned the sand and shell bits off the ping pong ball-shaped eggs. The eggs would only have to boil for a few minutes; the soft shell then allowed you to pinch a hole in it and suck the egg out. They would not hard boil so you could suck the egg right through the hole. Like most of the Lowcountry food ways that are governed by the seasons, this was a ritual we always looked forward to.

Thinking back, I am struck by the differences in how we were raised then as compared to now. Today, many of my cherished childhood memories would now attract the attention of a Game Warden or Child Protection Services. Nowadays, parents hover over their kids, afraid to let them explore the world around them. Our children are not expected to drink out of a water fountain anymore, much less a water hose. Perhaps times are not as safe now as they appeared back then...or it could be that we have grown more fearful of the world around us.

Chicken the Dog

The beaches of Charleston, Folly, Isle of Palms and Sullivan's Island, all have distinctively different feels about them. Folly has funky shops and surfer vibe, IOP with kid-friendly condos and ice-cream parlors, and finally Sullivan's, with what used to be quaint beach houses overlooking the harbor.

With me being the oldest of five boys, Mama would take the brood of us, at least those who could walk and hopefully not drown, to the beach. Always it seemed that some of her friends and their kids would tag along, sort of a Mothers' Morning Out, but with sand and bathing suits. Always accompanying us was the dog, a Weimaraner. His name was Chicken...please refrain from judging our unusual names here in the South.

We always went to the same part of the beach, like it was "our" place. I still find myself doing it today. Mama would establish our home base, and she and her girlfriends would arrange those aluminum and webbing chairs in a line to maximize exposure to the sun, and proceed to slather on the baby oil. Turkeys at Thanksgiving are roasted in much the same manner. This was in the 1960's and Coppertone had yet to make inroads into Southern customers' minds and retail locations. To this day I do not wear sunscreen.

Anyway, the platoon of kids would be in the water, splashing, yelling and throwing globs of sand at each other. Our mothers were up on the beach...gossiping, drinking sweet tea from a sweating glass carafe and smoking cigarettes. And our baby sitter was Chicken the dog.

He would be out in the surf, between us and the deeper water, acting like a cutting horse to prevent us from going out past our knees. If we did, a sharp bark and quick knockdown would be our reward for disobeying his authority. All the while, the mothers could carry on, secure in the knowledge that their "chillin's" were safe. During the summertime today, dogs are not allowed on beach and certainly not off leash! Perhaps the town council should reexamine this. Being babysat by a hound dog more attentive than most humans would surely allow some much-needed leisure time to Real Housewives of Mount Pleasant. More so, it leaves an indelible paw print in my memory of carefree fun with Chicken the Dog to look after us.

DAH AND YANKEES

The word Gullah refers to both descendants of black slaves who were brought to South Carolina to work initially in indigo and then in rice fields (because of their knowledge of planting and harvesting in humid environments), as well as their native language that evolved from a patois of English mixed with West Indies Caribbean sayings and pronunciation rules.

For many years in the Lowcountry, families would hire a Dah. In the Gullah way of life, a Dah was a glorified Nanny and actually head of the household. The Dah taught you your manners, how to sew, how to cook, and basically everything you would need to get through life. My grandmother had a Dah and her name was Georgiana Coakley Smith. My grandmother's name was Edith Guilds and everybody called her Edie. Everybody called Georgiana, Dah.

Dah started working for Edie when Edie was 6 months old and Dah was 13 years old. That was about the time when she started strolling Edie around in her perambulator and in general taking care of everyone. My great grandfather eventually built Dah her own house behind the big house and she lived there the rest of her life, Incidentally, my parents live in that same small house today.

At one point, Dah left for a few years but returned and lived behind Edie and Granddaddy's house for the remainder of their lives. Granddad died first and Edie died years later when she was 87 years old. At that time, Dah was 100 and had outlived her baby girl. Fours years later, Dah would rejoin Edie in heaven.

Understand, Dah did all of the cooking for Edie and Granddaddy. Edie was not in the kitchen that much, mostly because Dah wouldn't let her in there. It was her domain, and she would defend it against invaders, foreign and domestic. In fact, Dah conveyed her methods of cooking to only two people that I know of: my Mother when she married my Dad, and then onto me after she met Caddie.

As a newlywed, my Mother told me about Dah pulling her aside and saying, "Now this is how he likes his chicken and this is how he likes his shrimp (meaning my Dad)," and so on. When I graduated high school in 1976 I went to Maine to go to Bowdoin College. I met Carolyn, my future wife, the first day I was there. It wasn't too long before she informed me that we were getting married. Before you knew it, we had raised four kids in Maine. Everybody calls Carolyn, Caddie. It has been her nickname since college but that is a story for another occasion...and her permission to spill the details!

Back in 1978 I brought Caddie down to meet my family and spend time in Edie and Granddaddy's house. On meeting Caddie, Edie and Granddaddy whisked her off into the parlor which is where they always greeted their guests. As they left, and with Caddie looking back at me with a somewhat helpless look, I felt a vise-like grip on my arm. It's was Dah, marshaling me into her vestibule, the kitchen.

Once there, with a definiteness of a master passing the torch, she proceeded to educate me on how to fry chicken, how to fry shrimp and so on. I said nothing, afraid to muddle the directives with questions and thus break the spell. The secrets were shared succinctly with full gravitas. In my whirling mind, a conflict arose.

Caddie is from the Midwest, from Ann Arbor, Michigan. Growing up in Mount Pleasant, for some reason I was under the impression that yankees only came from New York. "Yankees" was not used as insult; rather a demarcation of geographic origin. If we wished to insult our brothers from northern climes, we simply label them "damnyankees"...one word.

After Dah finished with her lesson in the kitchen, I said, "Dah, why are you telling me all of this, I have been cooking since I was 12 years old?"

She very casually responded, "Because ain't no yankee can cook."

I pleaded "Dah, she ain't no yankee, she is from Ann Arbor, Michigan!"

She looked at me squarely in the eye and cooly says, "She ain't from around here."

Well Dah, you had me there, I guess. What she did not know, but in her aged prescience must have sensed, is that Caddie does not cook and never has. Dah's traditions and techniques, as is true with all Gullah traditions, have passed down through the generations. My boys have won medals in cooking using those same traditions.

Daniel Island

Visitors and citizens alike to Charleston are very familiar with the billboards promoting "The Good Life" on Daniel Island. The island is a massive planned community located on a tidal island in the middle of the Cooper River northeast of the City of Charleston. Now populated with million-dollar homes, a planned shopping and municipal center and a very relaxed yet organized life, the island was previously a sparsely inhabited enclave that would serve as wonderful playground for brave souls seeking to escape the heat of Charleston.

The major artery that runs the length of Charleston is Highway 17, spanning from Awendaw in the north, across the Peninsula (via the "Crosstown" as opposed to the formally named Septima P. Clark Parkway) and on to

Ravenel (the town, not the bridge). On our homestead off of Highway 17 North, we had a very large horse barn. There, my parents would provide boarding for up to 10 horses at a time for newly-arrived families who had just moved to town, and who happened to own horses, but no place to put them...sort of an Equine Self Storage, if you will.

Well, I am the oldest of five, and being obviously the most mature and responsible, it fell to me to feed the horses and muck the stalls. My brother Richard, who is just a year younger than me, was allergic to horses (so he claimed) and had to stay away from the barn...excepting those times of boyhood delight when he wanted to go shoot rats or ride one of the Shetland ponies. For some reason, I never was able to rationalize an allergy to horses with the ability to ride a pony. Actually, I still can't; remind me to revisit this with Richard at the next family reunion.

Anyway, several of the horses' owners would want some form of exercise for their horses in daycare . Consequently, I would take the horses for a spin around the area, up and down Highway 17 or up and down Longpoint Road, all in the name of a good lather, then take them back to the barn to wash them down and brush them.

Sometimes though, I would ride them up Longpoint Road to the intersection of Whipple and Longpoint. The road then turned to dirt and there was this little store/joint there on the right. It was called Ben's Grill. It was a white cinder block building that is still there today. The building now looks abandoned but back in the day, I could go in to buy a burger and a soda, or perhaps a couple of illicit beers and then continue riding on down the road. I was 12 or 13 at the time.

Well Longpoint Road continued on to the Wando River and to what is now the Wando Shipping Terminal. However, back then the road went through Mr. King's property along the river. At the end of the road, there were always a couple of little john boats..we used to call them "stump-jumpers". One in particular had a 15 horsepower Johnson motor on it and we (depending on who was hanging out at the store) would head to the landing, commandeer the boat and hop across to Daniel Island.

Unlike the master planned community that exists there today, there was nothing on Daniel Island except a couple of residents who prized their seclusion and a bunch of tick-infested deer. We could sit out there for hours, drinking cold beers, telling stories, and generally never worrying about anybody bothering us.

During our sojourns there, long before cell phones, my mother never knew exactly where I was and never really cared, as long as I was back at the house before dinner. She had this farm bell that we gave Dad one Christmas and when she rang that bell, you had 30 minutes to get home. First off, imagine that kind of adolescent freedom today, and then imagine being able to hear a bell ringing from Longpoint Road to Daniel Island! Mom and Dad gave me just enough freedom to know I was living.

The Grace Memorial bridge, connecting Charleston with Mount Pleasant, and predecessor to the Ravenel Bridge.

Long Point road, circa 1955

Guilds 1957 Chevrolet chariot from high school

Hibernian Hall, home of the St. Cecelia Ball

DEBUTANTE BALLS

Debutante balls once populated throughout the South, and reached their zenith in the city of Charleston. Most notably, the Saint Cecilia Society, recognized the city's leading young ladies being presented every year to society. Invitations to these events were more rare than to a president's inauguration, and Marshals who served at them considered themselves both fortunate and under a microscope, having the strictest rules of society and protocol to be observed at every occasion. Granted, an occasional slip of alcohol might have made its way into a punch bowl, and no doubt hilarity would have ensued .

Looking back, attending high school in Charleston in the early 1970's was an interesting experience. I went to Porter Gaud School, an all-boys school West of the Ashley River.

Many of the boys I went to school with lived in downtown Charleston. Now, as anyone who has familiarity with single-sex schools knows, there is often at least one, if not more, opposite-sex schools in close proximity, and Porter Gaud was no exception. Our gender counterpart was Ashley Hall, an all-girls school on Rutledge Avenue in downtown Charleston. Just like Porter Gaud, many of the girls who attended there also lived in downtown Charleston. And where there were collections of Southern girls back then, especially in South Carolina, there were Debutante Balls.

The debutante scene in Charleston was a very active one, but I had no early experience with it. Our home was out in the country; I just happened to go to school with that crowd. I remember in 9th grade I received an invitation in the mail to attend my first Debutante Ball. The R.S.V.P. directed me to "Please Contact Miss Charlotte".

I asked my mother what is this all about. In her wisdom, she explained that the St. Cecilia Society essentially orchestrated all of the debutante activities in Charleston. Consequentially, they also decided the pairing of the couples who would attend the Ball. I thought, "Wow! This is easy! They even tell you who you are going out with!" Oh how times have changed...

To the uninitiated, Debutante Balls carried the solemnity of a wedding without the actual "Death do us part". They were held in cloistered locations like Hibernian Hall, the Calhoun Mansion and other fancy places in the city of Charleston. Essentially, it was the occasion in which a young lady left her adolescence, and was presented to society. On rare occasions, two girls might share an event, but realistically, most of the balls would be for just one girl… I don't know how much was spent, but there was a full bar, caviar and all the fixins' with a full band. All you had to own was a tuxedo, always bought at Berlin's downtown, and you could eat and drink for free a couple of nights a week during the spring and fall seasons.

In addition to the Ball itself, there were also a series of cocktail parties almost every weekend before a girl made her debut...sort of like scrimmages, if you will. Charleston is always about two seconds from a party and the idea that you were making your debut gave them an excuse to throw another party. And in keeping with the intended exclusivity, it was usually the same people every weekend. Since I played music all through high school with my friend Dolph, we would many times be hired to play music for these cocktail parties. It wasn't a bad way to while away a weekend!

So the way the Ball would work is the party started at 7:00 in the evening for the adults to meet the debutante. Then the kids showed up at 9:00 and danced until 11:00. The bar somehow ended up being open most of the time and food was very plentiful. My routine of escorting Charlotte to these Balls was to pick her up around 7:00 at her house on Meeting Street on the corner of Meeting and Ladson. I would park my 1957 Chevy on the corner of Meeting and Ladson and make my way to the front door and ring the bell. Charlotte's Dad would answer the door and "us men" would go into the parlor which was right off the entry way on the left. We would talk about whatever he was in the mood to talk about. After the almost-mandatory-15-minute-time-delay, Charlotte would come down the stairs in her gown. We would hug, not too affectionately mind you, and head off to dinner, usually to the Harbor House or Colony House. After dinner we would head on up to the party. We would get there about 9:00 and spend the rest of the night dancing. We both loved to dance.

Well, this continued on for 3 and 1/2 years. But then the powers that be must have found out about some transgression I had committed (not entirely unbelievable). So in the spring of my senior year I received an invitation to one of the Balls and the invite directed me not to call on Charlotte, but on another girl staying at the Mills House. What happened to Charlotte?

Girls usually made their debut after their Freshman or Sophomore year in college so this meant that I was calling for this girl's friend from College. So anyway, I go ahead and make arrangements with the girl from the Mills House. I took her to dinner and stayed with my usual routine.

Well this is what happened with Charlotte. Her mother, who was a big player in the Charleston scene and Saint Cecilia Society, had apparently decided that I was now persona non gratis, and that it would be best for Charlotte (and her reputation) if she were escorted by Brian.

However, one thing that Charlotte's mother had not planned on was that Brian and I were close running buddies..sort of exchanging a Pontiac for a Buick, but they are both Chevys. But any way, this was Brian's routine that evening.

Brian and two friends went to Big John's Tavern on East Bay Street and enjoyed a few beers before the Ball. Feeling supremely confident, they showed up in front of Charlotte's house a little before 9:00...keep in mind I was always there at 7:00. Attempting to park his Plymouth Fury III as close as he could to the curb, he hit the large carriage stone that sat squarely on the sidewalk in front of the house. The stones are there from the old days of carriages and functioned as a mounting block to get up into and down out of a carriage, and their size and weight are impressive.

Well anyway, Brian honked the car's horn to announce his arrival, fully expecting Charlotte to bound down the stairs. It is not difficult to imagine that Charlotte's father was neither impressed nor amused. I don't know the exact conversation that took place inside, but eventually Charlotte made her appearance, and joined Brian and his friends in the car. Off to the party they went.

Soon after arriving, it was obvious that Brian was having fun and so was Charlotte. The only person not enjoying herself was Charlotte's mom. She was one of the chaperons that stayed late to make sure us kids didn't get into too much trouble. After a bit, Brian decided he wanted to dance on the stage with the band. Apparently demonstrating one of his patented dance moves, he ripped the inseam of his tuxedo pants. Completely unfazed, his solution was to take off his cummerbund and tie it around his thigh so as not to flash his boxer shorts to everyone present. Not dancing simply wasn't an option.

Enter Charlotte's mother. Describing her as "miffed" would be an understatement. She came up to me and asked, most sincerely and without a trace of irony, if I would mind making sure Charlotte got home safely. Being an upstanding Charleston gentleman, I said "Yes, Ma'am". All you really need to know how to say to make it in the Charleston society, or in life I have found is those 2 words, or whatever you call Ma'am.

So at 11:00 that night, I walked Charlotte up from Hibernian to her house on Meeting Street (I had already walked my date back to the Mills House which is right next door to Hibernian). Charlotte and I said goodnight and I headed back down to Hibernian to see what kind of trouble Brian might be in. But the trouble had yet to put in a full appearance.

On collecting him, we made the wise decision to walk back to his house on Ashley Avenue, as he (and I) might have enjoyed a few beverages and therefore might have been suffering from altered judgment.

On the way to his house, we saw a large street sweeper just idling on the street. I don't know what the driver was doing but he was not around. So we decided this was the perfect opportunity for a road trip to Savannah. Savannah is only 110 miles south of Charleston and by driving there we thought we could provide a valuable public service of scrubbing Highway 17 South clean. Understand, in those days, the top speed for a street sweeper was about about 3 miles an hour. Needless to say, we made it to Lockwood Drive and decided it was going to take way too much time, time we didn't want to spare that evening. We abandoned the sweeper and walked the remaining quarter of a mile back to his house. Hopefully the statute of limitations has passed. Two guys in tuxedos driving a street sweeper must have been a hell of a sight, but in Charleston we do it right!

Farm Bells

Drawing from it's colonial roots, the farm bell was a fixture in many Southern farm stands. Long before the days of mobile phones, or any type of phone for that matter, bells were rung to call neighbors, alert to a fire, or for many who grew up in the country, to signal a return home for suppertime after out gallivanting in the evenings.

When I was in high school, my Mother bought a big farm bell for Dad for Christmas. My brother Richard and I borrowed the company truck and went into town to pick up the bell from the Purina supply store. To keep it a secret, we planned on hiding it at a friend's house by the name of Coleman.

Coleman lived right up Highway 17 from us so it would be easy to retrieve on Christmas Eve. Now Coleman worked as a docking master for the tugboat company. A docking master is the person who climbs up on the ship from the tugboat and takes over from the harbor pilot who brings the ship into the harbor. Coleman was a big man, and I mean big like a bear. It was amazing to watch as he climbed up onto the ship. The tug and ship are probably going 5 knots and he would just lean an aluminum extension ladder up against the ship and scurry right on up. Coleman probably weighed 300 pounds.

Anyway, it was all Richard and I could do to load the bell into the truck because it too weighed about 300 pounds if not a little more. We drove it over to Coleman's house and he came out to meet us. We let the tailgate down and Coleman just matter-of-factly reached in and picked up the bell and put it down on the ground. I couldn't believe what I saw.

Christmas Eve, while we were at church, Coleman brought the bell over and put it on the back porch. My grandfather from Beaufort, Papa Jim, had come to visit us for Christmas but he didn't go to church with us so he knew about the bell. Christmas morning, the whole house was startled awake because Papa Jim decided it was time for everybody to get up so he started banging on the bell. It was 6:00 in the morning and at least a couple of us were in high school and 6:00 was entirely too early. Not for Papa Jim though; he was a shrimper from Frogmore, a small town across the river from Beaufort and he was already anxious to get back on the road home. We come stumbling downstairs to see what in the world is going on. Papa Jim has already fried bacon and sausage and made a pot of grits. He wanted to get going and soon. Once we left home and the house was sold, a childhood friend of Dad's took it and moved it to Silk Hope Plantation.

I think about Coleman and that bell and it makes me think of a place called Richard's. Richard's is a bar which still exists and Coleman and some of his other buddies from the waterfront hung out there. At that time Richard's had a corner of the bar with free weights in it. It was rather convenient to grab a few cool beers and knock out your workout in one visit.

I remember once being in there and there was a barbell on the floor with 325 pounds on it. The guys were drinking and someone that we didn't know was sort of poking at Brantley, a friend of Coleman's who was sitting beside him at the bar. The stranger looked at the barbell, looked at Brantley and said "I'll bet you $25 you can't pick that up."

Coleman gave a sideways smile towards Brantley. Probably because Brantley was even bigger than Coleman. Anyway, Brantley walks over to the weight and looks at it for a second then leans over and picks the weight up to his waist. He looks over at this heckler, and says, "For another $25, I'll put it over my head." The heckler paid his tab and left the bar. Needless to say, Brantley and Coleman could do anything they wanted in Richard's. When you come out to the country to play, you better just make sure you have your manners.

FOOTBALL

Competing with the Episcopal and Catholic churches for hearts and minds is the long honored religion of Football. Young men typically train in some capacity nine months of the year to represent their schools' Banner underneath the Friday Night Lights, All in hopes of one day pursuing that hallowed road that leads to the University of South Carolina or Clemson University. Even today Charleston boasts one of the top high schools in the state for football, Wando High School.

I grew up playing football. I don't really know why but beginning in 4th grade, I played every year. I guess it was just something you did. I started off playing Pee Wee league over on Sullivan's Island on the fields behind the fort. In high school, I played all four years. I went to

Porter Gaud and we were a small all-boys school. There were only 250 students in the whole high school and we were playing these AAA teams like Fort Johnson and Goose Creek and Bonds Wilson and North Charleston who had 1,000-2,000 students.

It really didn't make any sense but I played left offensive tackle and linebacker, weighing all of 160 pounds soaking wet. My brother Richard was the left guard and not much bigger. The kids I was playing against were all 250 pounds and had one goal in mind, which was to kill me. I guess that worked to our advantage because we ran the triple option. All the quarterback had to do was come down the line and hand it off to the running back or keep it. The choice was usually an easy one because all the defensive guy wanted to do was hurt me. He was so distracted trying to run me over that he would not even notice the running back coming through the line, and a first down was payment for sacrificing my life and limb.

I probably had four concussions throughout my high school years. One that sticks out in my mind, was while playing a game against Bishop England High School. Bishop England was a big rival and they especially liked to try to see just how much they could hurt us. This one particular play was just before half time and we were punting to Bishop England. I used to snapped the ball on the punts and the normal routine was as soon as I snapped the ball, someone on defense would hit me in the head with his forearm trying to knock me out. Well, it worked this time.

The rest of this particular story I saw on game films because I don't remember anything.

On this play, Number 48 for Bishop England, Derrick Hughes, was receiving the kick. He was a *big* guy. And after a defensive lineman hit me in the head, I started right down the middle of the field. Derrick looks to his right and left and sees that the smallest guy out there was me. Naturally, he headed right for me. He hit me straight on and even though I managed to grab him and tackle him, he flipped me straight over backwards.

At half time, we were in the end zone and according to Richard, my brother, I was very nauseous, which was highly unusual. He told Coach that something wasn't right with me but Coach just growled "Suck it up, Hollowell!".

Well he put me back in starting the second half and it didn't work out well. According to the game films, one of the first plays, Our Porter Gaud quarterback came down the left side of the line and I stood up to tackle him. My own quarterback. Needless to say coach took me out of the game.

My father came down and got me to the locker room. He helped me clean up and get dressed and on the way home with dad and Richard in the car, all I could ask was, "Who won the game? What was the score?". Richard and I shared a bedroom and on Saturday morning I woke up and the first thing I asked was, “Who won the game? What was the score?” Richard threw a book at me!

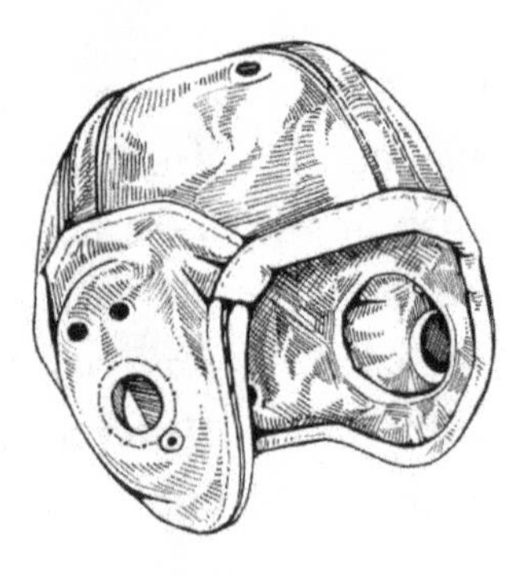

My junior year we actually beat Fort Johnson and they were the previous year’s state champions. I remember they threw this Hail Mary pass in the last seconds, and a very tall receiver hauled it in. But we pushed and pushed and he landed about 3 feet short of the goal line. We won 17-14. They were livid, and would not forget.

My senior year we headed over to Fort Johnson to play them on their home field and they killed us. That game sticks out in my head because the defensive tackle I had to block was number 74, Mike Slaughter. What an appropriate name. He beat me up for four quarters. He was quick, strong and I couldn’t do anything to block him. Coach got so mad at me, at half time he really let loose on me.

"Hollowell, dammit, you have to keep him out of our backfield!!"

I thought, "You try!"

But Mike was great and more interested in getting the ball than tackling me, which was different for a change. Needless to say we lost that game by an embarrassing margin which time has gratefully forgotten.

I graduated and headed north to go to school in Brunswick, Maine at Bowdoin College. One of the first weeks I was there a group of us were watching college football and it was a Clemson game. Back in the 1970's the television used to show an up close and personal picture of the players. Well sure enough, Mike Slaughter got a full scholarship to Clemson and he was the starting right defensive tackle for Clemson. When they flashed his picture it made me shutter, I got goose bumps. At least I got beat up by that sort of talent. That was football for me in high school! I don't know if it was discipline or foolishness, but I lived to tell about it.

Gervais and the Nova

Charlestonians have always prized a certain measure of exclusivity to their society. One example of this is their naming and pronunciation of certain words. Huger Street is not pronounced the way it would seem, but instead is pronounced "U-G". A very familiar family name in Charleston is Gervais, which is not pronounced the way it is spelled, instead being "Jer-vay". Even cockroaches, quite common here, are called "Palmetto bugs". It's one of the ways someone "not from here" can be quickly identified!

I am the oldest of five boys and the fourth one down is named Gervais. Growing up, Gervais loved to go off-roading. One problem...he never had a four-wheel drive vehicle. What Gervais drove was a two-door, green Chevy

Nova and Gervais thought he could take that car anywhere. He just figured if he went really fast he could get through anything. That car had a dent in every panel of the body.

One night there was a party being hosted on the U.S.S. Yorktown and while Gervais didn't get to go, a bunch of his buddies did. It was a formal affair and all the guys were wearing tuxedos and the girls wearing their gowns. Some of the guys decided to leave the party a little early and go out four-wheeling. They were just starting to build the Patriots Point golf course so all the construction equipment was out there and it was muddy. It was raining and Gervais had gone out there to spy on the party.

He finds his friends in their Jeeps riding through the mud with their tuxedos on and the girls in their gowns. I guess it wasn't long before a couple of them got stuck and they didn't have a way to get out so Gervais decided to go out and see if he could find some help.

Heading back out to the highway, there was mud on his headlights; add the rain, and Gervais couldn't quite see where he was going. He was coming out from the construction site and thought he was taking the road out but instead drove right into a ditch. So Gervais got out, walked up to the gas station and called me at home. I was down visiting from Maine on Christmas break.

It was probably around 11:30 at night and I drove over to Patriot's Point. There is the Nova, nose-first in the ditch with the back wheels off the ground by about two or three inches.

Gervais looked at me with a very serious look on his face, and said "If we can just get the back wheels to touch the ground, I'm pretty sure I can back it out of the ditch." I have never laughed so hard. I told him if he could make that happen, General Motors would give him a new car. A tow truck finally removed the Nova, and everybody eventually made it home. But to see two Jeeps buried in the mud and the Nova in the ditch, almost straight up and down, was a sight I'll never forget. You have to admire anyone with that much faith.

Gus Qualls & BB Guns

It is the rare Southern born Native Son who does not at some point in his childhood dream of earning glories through military service. As an outgrowth of this desire, and another due to a young man's desire to seek out dangerous activities, many young men practice their mock war games with spears or swords (or anything that will substitute as a sword, such as a yard stick or even a yard rake handle), and finally graduating to the use of BB guns to storm pretend beachheads and defend tree forts.

When I was 9 years old my parents bought Snee Farm. Now they didn't buy the whole farm; they just bought the farmhouse and barn. All together it was about 20 acres. It was originally Charles Pinckney's house built back in 1754. The fellow they bought it from was the former ambassador to the Netherlands from Canada, Ambassador Stone, and he used the house for his getaway and hunting lodge. After he died the estate sold the house to Dad and the rest was leased to a local farmer. The rest of the farm was about 900 acres and it was all tomato and cucumber fields.

There were three people living right up the road who used to work for the Ambassador when he would come down so they were used to being around the house. One of them was Gus Qualls. Gus didn't work for my parents but he would come around the house all the time. For my birthday one year Mom and Dad gave me a BB gun. I was all excited, the way any young man would be with such a gift.

One day I was out in the yard shooting cans or something and Gus came around.

He said "Let me see that."

So I gave him the gun and he says "Now run! RUN!"

What did he mean?!? So I started out across the yard and Gus started shooting at my legs with the BB gun. It scared me half to death. But after I was out of range, I thought this was sort of fun. Strange times, indeed.

The woman who worked for my mother was named Rosalee and she had a few kids. They would come around with their friends and we would have BB gun wars. Back in the 60's, kids may have played war games because the

Vietnam War was all over the news. We had rules for the BB gun wars. No shooting above the waist was the biggest one. Trying to hit someone running across the field with a BB gun is not easy. But we might have two teams of six people each playing at a time. It really was a lot of fun.

I went to a private boys school over west of the Ashley, Porter Gaud School and it was an all-boys school with most of the kids coming from downtown Charleston. Sometimes my mother would take me to town to play with the kids I went to school with. They also played war games but the difference is they used sticks as fake guns. I think they spent more time arguing over whether or not they got hit than actually playing the game.

So I said, "Y'all should come over to my house if you want to see real war games."

So eventually a few of them made it out. Back then, it was a real hike to get all the way to Snee Farm. But when they did make it out, I introduced them to my friends from up the road and they all brought their BB guns. Well my friends from town didn't know what to do or say, but they played anyway. They realized that when you got hit with a BB, you didn't have to argue, it hurt! They would go home with welts on their legs but usually smiling. When their mothers would ask mine about the welts, mom would just blame it on chiggers from the Spanish moss. I don't know if my mother was just not paying attention or just didn't care but we would sometimes leave the house in August wearing two pair of jeans and long sleeve shirts just to avoid the big welts. Anyway, all that I learned from Gus. You tend to grow up pretty fast living and hanging out in the country.

Snee Farm and the bell

The Hollowell family

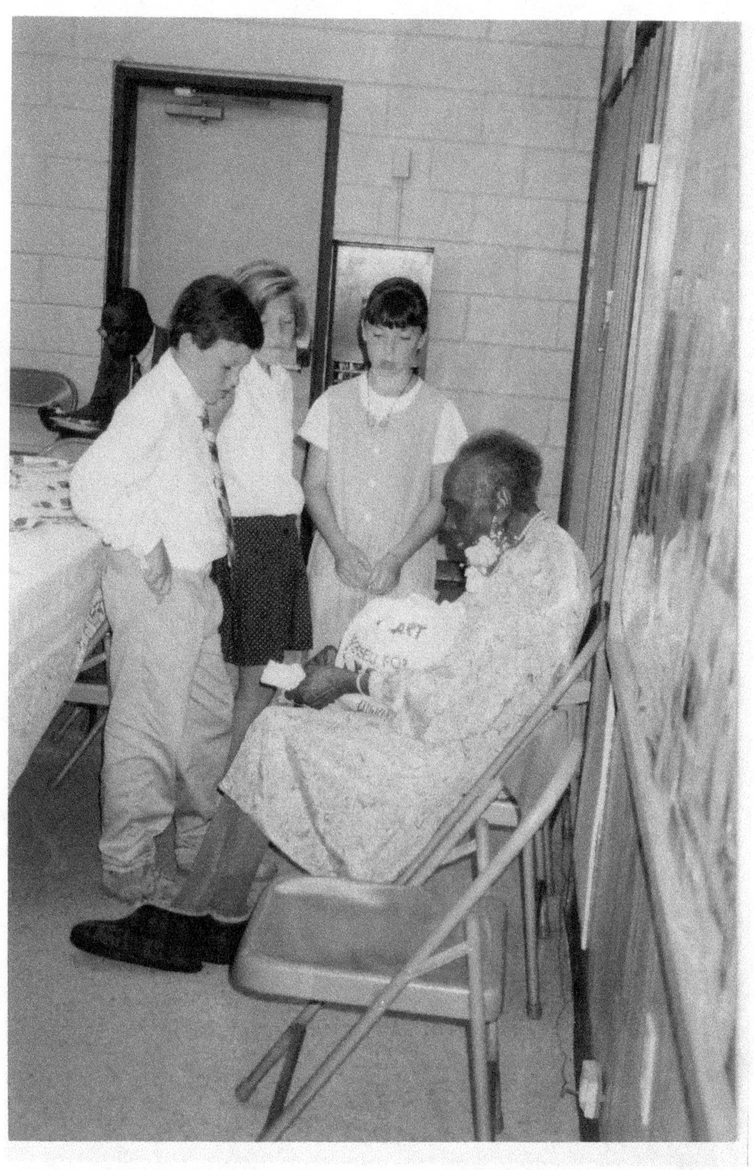

Dah spending time with the Guy and Brock Hollowell and friend Harriett at Dah's 100th birthday party

Harry and the Barges

Initially, Charleston topography as a peninsula at the joining of the Ashley and Cooper (some say Charleston is where the Ashley and Cooper meet to form the Atlantic Ocean) was ringed with wharfs on both sides of the city, underlining the importance of ocean shipping to the city. Even today, barges transport cargo both north and south via the protected Intracoastal waterways, as well as massive cargo ships docking at the Charleston docks on East Bay and the Wando shipping terminal.

When I was working at Seahol Contracting, I had an opportunity to work for a couple of summers bunkering barges. This is filling a barge with oil and taking it somewhere to off load it. Sometimes I would off load up at Bushy Park in Goose Creek to the power plant and sometimes I would bunker a ship which is basically filling it with fuel, from the barge. The person I learned this from was named Harry. Harry was sort of crazy but he got the job done, and taught me a thing or two, whether I wanted to learn it or not.

If you have ever seen barges that ferry crude oil, you can imagine they have no smoking signs all over: No Smoking, Flammable, No Smoking-Flammable, etc. Basically the same kind of signs you would see at a gas station. I usually loaded barges at the Exxon dock but would offload them at many different ships or docks up the Cooper River. I would go up as far as Bushy Park or anywhere in between. When you unload a barge, you unload the front tanks before the back tanks, kind of like emptying a glass. So the pump runs faster on the front tanks than the back tanks and you monitor the oil level in each tank. As the front tanks go down you increase the speed of the back tanks and slow down the front tanks.

When you look down into the tank, especially when it is dark, there is virtually no light, and really only a reflection from inside the tank. So you can't really tell where the oil level is unless you can create a ripple or something to show the level of the oil in the tank. To create the ripple, you spit in it and it creates a little ripple and then from that ripple you count how many steps you can see in the tank and figure out how much oil has been pumped. But this is not the way Harry did it.

The very first time Harry taught me how to check the level of the oil in the tank, I have to admit I was a little scared.

Harry was walking around the barge with a cigarette hanging out of his mouth and the signs, of course, clearly saying No Smoking. He didn't care at all.

Well we got up to the tank and he said "Lean in, boy! and I am going to show you how to count these steps."

So he took his lit cigarette from his mouth and threw it in the tank. I repeat...threw the cigarette in the tank!

At this point, I made an instantaneous decision to rapidly leave the barge. I started running for the edge of the barge, thinking this thing was blowing up! Man, there were flammable signs everywhere!

All this time, Harry is laughing his head off at me. Come to find out, you can't light crude oil with a blowtorch, much less a cigarette, but it was scary just the same.

This was my first introduction into bunkering barges, and while I did spend a couple of summers working on the barges, I never had the guts to throw a cigarette in the tank. I had many experiences working for Seahol that you just chalk up to another chapter in life.

Henry's Crabs

Despite its fearsome appearance and aggressive nature, the blue crab is greatly cherished in the South Carolina Lowcountry. Gourmets prefer the blue crab's sweet meat over all other locally caught seafood. Blue crabs require both inshore brackish waters and high salinity ocean waters to complete their life cycle. The blue crab's scientific name, Callinectes sapidus, translates to "savory beautiful swimmer." Large males, called Jimmies by fishermen, have brilliant blue claws and legs. The mature females, or "sooks," have bright orange tips on their claws.

I have a friend named Henry who lived in Hanahan, South Carolina, north of Charleston. After I graduated Porter Gaud I went up to Maine to go to college. I think it was during a school break when I was visiting for a couple of days that I ran into Henry downtown, probably at Big John's.

We shook hands and I said "Henry, how you doing?"

"Not so good," he said, "I have had a hell of a day."

After high school, Henry and a buddy named Charlie lived on a little farm up in Hollywood. Henry's brother was a crab fisherman and so Henry decided to open up a crab picking factory on the property. He would hire the pickers and pay them by giving them a bushel of crab for every bushel they would pick. Everything was going along well and so Henry and Charlie decided that since they had all of these crab shells and scraps, why not raise some pigs? Pigs will eat anything and they had plenty of something they could feed them. So they started raising some pigs and feeding them the scraps.

Everything was going along great so Henry decided he was going to double his capacity for cooking the crabs by getting a pressure cooker. He could cook 12 bushels of crabs in the pressure cooker as quick as he could cook 6 bushels in an open pot.

Well, everybody from around here knows that you cook crab in an open pot. That way the haints or the evil spirits can get out of the pot. You know his pickers were not happy about this pressure cooker, it was just not right.

The day I saw Henry, he was in town trying to forget his awful day. It seems he had taken one of his pigs to market and had come into town to collect the money for the pig. Well come to find out, his pig tasted a lot like crab and there was no market for crab/pig or pig/crab. You are what you eat and in this case it backfired.

So he was upset about that but when he got back to his farm, all of his pickers were outside in the field on their hands and knees praying to God.

Henry said, "Guilds, I walked in the shop and the pressure cooker had exploded. There were pieces of crab claws and shells all in the walls and ceiling. I had to give everybody a few days off and so I decided to come into town. It has been a bust of a week and a hell of a day." Some days just don't work out like you plan. I guess life is what happens while you are busy making plans.

JOKER LOUNGE

Charleston's location and ever present sailing and naval community has brought homesick sailors to our shores since the founding of the colony in the 1600's. As is wont to occur when these men hit the shore, bars and other dens of iniquity such as strip clubs made their appearance. The Joker Lounge was one of these hangouts from back in the day. Nowadays, Charleston has gentrified itself, and pushed these somewhat unsavory elements to the outer borders of the city.

I have a good friend named Brian. He and I spent a great deal of time playing pool in Big John's (many a story from many a Charlestonian began with the words "I was at Big John's..."). If I wasn't playing music or golf somewhere or working on the barges, chances are I was with Brian. Back in my high school days, the blue laws in South Carolina made the bars close at midnight. The drinking age was 18, not that it really mattered.

My mother's law was that if I was not going to be home by midnight, I had to call and let her know. So every night around 11:45, I would find a pay phone and call her to let her know I would be a little later. While the bars closed at midnight, the private clubs stayed open until 2:00 a.m. After Big John's closed, Brian and I would sometimes head up to the Joker Lounge, a strip club on upper Meeting Street. Neither one of us were big on the strippers but there was an act there that was our favorite. Her name was Big Mama. She was the woman who coordinated all of the dancers and late in the evening she might do her dance if she was asked often enough.

Well, Brian and I would sit by the stage and holler for Big Mama until she would come out. She was a vary large black woman and wore a black leotard with glow in the dark tassels on each breast and on each butt cheek. She could make those tassels all go in the same direction, stop one tassel, and keep the others going, make them go in opposite directions, pretty much whatever she wanted. It was amazing and Brian and I would just sit there hooting and hollering just to cheer her on.

To this day, I still can't believe she could make those tassels stop on a dime and go in any direction she wanted.

Anyway, after the show I'd make my way home and go in to tell Mom I was home. Dad would always be asleep and more often than not I would wake up Mom to let her know I was safe. Not sure why this made us both feel better but it did. But like a good Charleston son, I never told her about going to the Joker Lounge...until now!

ROAD KILL

Today, Charleston is the home of world class cuisine and several James Beard award winners and nominees. But this has not always been the case. Early cookbooks recognize the original local food fare such as possums and snapping turtles and even raccoon! The famous Charleston cookbook Charleston Receipts was even preceded by a much less well-known book known as Charleston's Recipes, which was populated with many of the local country recipes that made excellent use of flora and fauna around Charleston. Growing up in the South, my mother even loved armadillo, which she called "possum on the half shell."

The woman who worked for my mother to help with the 5 of us was Rosalee Robinson. She had a girl and a few boys herself and we spent time together. She lived just up the road and whether she drove or walked to work, she knew Longpoint Road and all of the new, fresh roadkill.

One day Rosalee came over to the house. I think on this occasion she didn't expect anybody to be home. She had found a possum on the road that was still warm and she brought it to the house. One of the girls who used to work for the Ambassador also lived just up the road. Her name was Maggie and Rosalee called her to come pick up the possum.

I was up at Snee Farm Country Club waiting on my tee time for some tournament and I had forgotten something and came running back to the house. Now one of the ways to get into the house was to come in the side door and right when you walked in, there were two sets of steps; you could take the steps down into the basement or steps going up into the kitchen.

That day, Rosalee had taken the possum she had found and laid it out on the second or third step going up into the kitchen. I went racing through that door and I grabbed the post to launch myself up the stairs and there was this possum, dead, feet up in the air, teeth bared, just looking at me. It scared the hell out of me and I turned around in midair. I am pretty sure I didn't touch anything as I went right back out the door. And truth be told, I wet my pants.

I had to go back out to the front door of the house and went upstairs so I could change my clothes, I almost missed my tee time and as I was running back out the house I said, "Rosalee you know there is a dead possum on the stairs?"

She said, "I know. Maggie is going to get 'em and clean em". Just as casual as you can be.

Anyway, Maggie must have come and gotten that possum because by the time I came back from playing golf the possum was gone. Thank God. Rosalee was an amazing influence for me. Growing up in a predominately Gullah environment with Rosalee taught me that the basics are all you really need. I never did take a liking to possum though!

Rosalee with Guilds' son, Guy

Guilds showing off his “assets” at a pep rally

VOL. 161, No. 180 ★ ★ TELEPHONE RA 2-5522

(Staff Photo By Knisely)

Army Reservists Leave For Training In New Orleans

Specialist 2-c Guilds Hollowell of Mount Pleasant gets a salute from his wife and sons as he departs for a two-week tour of training duty in New Orleans. A 14-car troop train departed here yesterday carrying 320 Lowcountry U. S. Army Reserve personnel. Three Charleston Transportation Corps units were joined on the Atlantic Coast Line special train by the 389th Transportation Battalion of Florence. A fifth unit, the 348th Terminal Unit of Savannah, Ga., boarded the train in the Georgia city last night. The 65-man strong U. S. Army Terminal Unit will direct the units in summer exercises. Other Charleston units are the 453rd Transportation Co., with 129 men, and the 942nd Transportation Co., 97 men.

Mama, Guilds and his brother Richard waving goodbye to their father.

ROBY HUFFMAN

Charleston's early history shows it to be one of the most integrated and progressive cities in America before the War Between the States. This changed after the war and Reconstruction. The Ku Klux Klan was born from defeated and disgruntled Confederates, to grow into a powerful terrorist militia that even the Governor was intimidated by. The situation in South Carolina grew so dire that President Ulysses S. Grant and Congress passed the Ku Klux Klan Act in 1871, outlawing the Klan, and driving it underground for almost 100 years.

Music has always been a big part of my life. I started playing guitar when I was about 11 or 12 and when I was 14 or so I met Dolph. Dolph played the banjo and we would meet up and play around town a good bit. We also took some road trips up to North Carolina to visit some of the bluegrass festivals up there. His Dad lived up close to Wilson, North Carolina and there was a festival held up in that part of North Carolina in a town called Smithfield. Smithfield was a tiny little town probably about 8,000-10,000 people.

Coming into town was interesting because there was this billboard that was probably 60 feet high welcoming you to Smithfield. On the top of the billboard it said, "Welcome to Smithfield, home of the KKK". I had heard of the KKK through movies but never experienced a community that called itself the “Home of the KKK”.

Well, the festival that year was a blast and we met a guy named Roby Huffman. He was an amazing tenor singer and he had a band called Roby Huffman and the Bluegrass Cutups. He was a big time name in Eastern North Carolina.

Dolph and I decided my junior year that we were going to throw a big square dance and invite all of the kids and parents of both Porter Gaud and Ashley Hall high school. We decided we were going to ask Roby to come down with his band and he accepted the offer.

He had never been to Charleston and was excited to see it. We held the party at The South Carolina National Guard Armory in Mt. Pleasant on Mathis Ferry Road. The day of the party was exciting. The armory was decorated and many of the parents had chipped in to help. Dolph and I had plans to show Roby and the group around town before the square dance. We were going to take them out to Fort Sumter and down around the battery. Well they didn't show up when they said they would. They weren't late for the party but they were a few hours later than planned. It didn't really matter to them because all the way down from Smithfield they had been drinking rum and Coke. Of course it was a couple bottles of rum and a 6-ounce bottle Coke I am pretty sure. Anyway, all they wanted to do was get their picture taken sitting on the cannon and next to the tank out front of the armory .

Well the party got going and everybody was having a grand time. The turnout was great and the party was about 50/50 students and parents. My mother had helped with the decorations and was equally enjoying herself. Incidentally, the manager of the band was also at the party and having a good ol' time. I didn't know him well but I had heard that not only was he in the KKK, but he was the Grand Dragon up in Smithfield. He seemed like a nice guy... but also a Grand Dragon.

An hour or so into the party, my mother came up to me and said." Guilds, do you know this young man? He is so nice".

It was the manager of the band. My mother was probably 40 years old and an attractive woman. He was close to her age.

She said to me, “He is going to take me out to show me the band’s bus”.

I laughed out loud and said, “Mom, I need some help over here at the food table.”

My mother was from Lady's Island, South Carolina and a little naive. I don’t know what might have happened, if anything, but at the time I thought it best she not get too comfortable with the guy!

So this was my experience with the great Roby Huffman and the Bluegrass Cutups. I never knew what became of the band manager, but Roby died in 2012 as a legend in Eastern North Carolina.

Rockville Regatta

The Rockville Regatta, now in its 126-year and occurring in August, is one of Charleston's two sailing "anchor" events, along with Charleston Race Week in the spring. It isn't the biggest regatta in the Charleston lowcountry with only 40 to 50 boats at a time, but it's long history makes Rockville a special place as the area's open regatta season wraps up. Hundreds of spectator boats usually fill the waters across from Sea Island Yacht Club in what some call the world's largest floating cocktail party. "Rockville has always taken place the first full weekend in August," says Grayson Carter, the immediate past commodore and current treasurer of Sea Island Yacht Club. "Rockville was a place for the people who lived in Charleston, who lived on Johns Island and Wadmalaw Island, to congregate and escape the heat of the summer,

a place to be able to cool off, be near the water and enjoy the sea breeze."

I was never a big sailor but my dad owned a Widgeon and I would sail in local regattas in the Charleston area with him. Mount Pleasant had a Widgeon regatta every year, and we would put our boat in at the foot of King Street in Mount Pleasant and just sail around buoys on the Mount Pleasant side of Crab Bank.

I did attend a few regattas just for the party. One of the biggest parties in the Lowcountry is the Rockville regatta. Rockville is a little community on Wadmalaw Island and it has a building right on the creek that is the Sea Island Yacht Club.

The regatta itself was not a huge regatta, but the party was one of the biggest in the season. There might've only been three dozen sailboats actually participating in the regatta, but there were three times that many boats floating around for the party that came afterwards. This one particular regatta was my senior year in high school I believe, but it might have been my junior year.

The usual sailing crowd was out there but there was a boy named David who had a brand-new speedboat; it was a Glastron. Most of the guys this part of town used to play with Boston Whalers and that type of boat in the river, but David had this fancy purple speckled speedboat. He loved to race up and down the river showing off his boat. There was another guy named Penrod, and Penrod was probably in his early 40s. Penrod brought out his own homemade wooden boat.

Now this wasn't just a normal boat. First off, anybody who's been around Charleston for any length of time knew Penrod. He really approached the edge of being a little crazy. So his boat was a homemade wooden boat and the engine was a 454 Chrysler engine. I think it was a Chrysler, or whoever made a 454 engine back in the 70s. It had a steering wheel and instead of the throttle it had an accelerator, the gas pedal like in a car. It had a four barrel carburetor; it was a fast little boat.

Well David was all excited about his new boat and how fast it was, so he decided he was going to challenge Penrod to a little race. David got scooting up the river and I don't how fast he was going, maybe 40 miles an hour. I don't know how fast is *fast* in those things, but David was heading down the river at a pretty good pace.

Well Penrod eases on up next to David. He just smiled, then he puts his foot down on the floor on that gas pedal and all four barrels on the carburetor kicked in. There was a screaming noise that you wouldn't believe; it threw up a rooster tail and it sent water all over David's boat. Penrod just laughed. Then, just to finish the game, once Penrod proved that he had beaten David, he would just throw it into reverse. Water came back up into the boat and flooded the entire boat. We would bail it out and do it all over again.

The Rockville Regatta was always an interesting party. They eventually built a cyclone-fenced area, maybe ten yards square but the fence was only about 4 feet high. That was the "jail". When people acted up, instead of having to take them to the James Island jail, they just fenced them in until they sobered up. Rockville wasn't just a party, it was an unforgettable event each year.

SNEE FARM AND MOM

Mount Pleasant's Snee Farm Plantation was listed on the National Register of Historic Places as a National Historic Landmark in 1973. This plantation has a rich and diverse history spanning three centuries. The original property was a 500-acre land grant given to Richard Butler in 1696. Long Point Road was established along the northern boundary of Butler's property around 1707. In 1738, Benjamin Law transferred the land to John Allen who acquired additional parcels totaling 715 acres by 1744. After Allen died, his widow sold the parcel to Col. Charles Pinckney on Sept. 17, 1754. Col. Pinckney was the father of one of America's founding fathers, Charles Pinckney, Jr. In May 1791, George Washington ate breakfast at Snee Farm under a huge oak. A silver spoon

he may have used was found during restoration of the Pinckney house in the 1930's, and donated by Joyce Hollowell, a later owner, to the National Park Service. After breakfast, Washington took a ferry to Charles Town. He was greeted in the harbor by a boat carrying the St. Michael's choir, and met on land by dignitaries including Governor Charles Pinckney, Jr.

In 1967, I was 9 years old. That year, my parents bought Snee Farm; not the whole farm, just the farmhouse and barn and about 20 acres. The other 900 plus acres were cucumber fields. They bought it from the estate of former Ambassador Stone. He was the Ambassador to the Netherlands from Canada and Snee Farm was his hunting lodge. Snee Farm was a very magical place to grow up.

A couple of years after we moved in, an insurance company started developing a golf course and today it is Snee Farm Country Club. My house is called the Charles Pinckney Historic Site and it is a National Park. I think if you know anybody who graduated from Porter Gaud or Ashley Hall in the mid to late 70's or early 80's, they might remember some of the parties out at Snee Farm. We lived on the other side of nowhere and so many times people would just spend the night. You could sleep at least 20 in the hayloft at the barn.

When I was 12 or 13, I started doing some work for the country club. I would sweep the lines on the tennis courts and help bring the golf carts up from the cart barn. They were electric carts. Since I had the keys to the cart barn, sometimes we would go up and borrow some golf carts for a little while and have cart races around the yard and the paddocks. We always put them up at the end of the night, but sometimes the end of the night was a little too late and they wouldn't charge enough and would be sluggish the next day. Charlie, the golf pro, would ask me if we had had a power outage that night and I would usually say "We must have! Who knows, we are way out in the country after all!"

Now, as you know by now, I am the oldest of 5 boys and I know we drove my Mama crazy. As we started getting into high school, we got a little crazier. I drove a 1957 Chevy and it was painted maroon and white, maroon being one of the Porter Gaud school colors.

I remember times we would tie a piece of plywood flat to the back of the car to drag it around the horse paddock. It was the favorite game of "Crack the Whip", or another way for boys to try to hurt themselves, slinging each other around a paddock! I don't know if my Mom just didn't notice or if she even cared, but we would run out of the house dressed in jeans and long sleeve shirts with rubber bands around the wrists and ankles. That was to keep the fire ants out if you hit them in the field.

This one time, my brother Richard was on the plywood and we were flying. I know when I made the turn around the corner of the paddock I was going at least 30 mph. Richard was whipping around the corner and had to be going faster than that. As we turned the corner, I was looking forward at the front porch of the house and I could see Richard in my rear-view mirror. Just then, my Mother walks out on the porch and all I can see is her screaming something. Right then, Richard fell off the plywood and bounces a couple of times right into the paddock fence. He collapsed to the ground and twitched a little, sort of a little shake.

I don't remember who was in the car but we made the decision that Richard would be just fine, however, we were smart enough to know to get out of there and avoid Mom. So we drove out of the paddock and went over to the barn. When we came back a little bit later, Richard was fine and Mom had calmed down enough so we knew so she wouldn't throttle us within an inch of our lives. She wouldn't have hurt us obviously, but it would not have been too pretty!

There were many incidents like that and I will share one more with you. It was pear season and we had a small pear orchard of maybe a dozen trees. Mom wanted us to go pick the pears. Now, you couldn't just shake the tree and gather them, (she didn't want them bruised) so you had to get into the tree and pick the pears. It was a pain in the neck.

Well we procrastinated too much and one day on our way home from school, we turned into the driveway. The driveway was maybe 80 yards from the house and as we turned in we heard the "Boom! Boom!," shots from a shotgun.

Mom was standing there, shooting the crows out of the pear trees. We immediately turned around and head back out. One of my brothers asked, "How many shells were in the closet?" We just wanted to make sure she had run out of ammo before we went back to the house.;.. just in case.

My Mom grew up on Lady's Island, South Carolina and her Dad was a shrimper. He had taught her how to shoot a gun but I guess she had forgotten some of it because the next day her shoulder was black and blue. I could go on forever with stories, but you can understand a little bit why Snee Farm was such a unique place to grow up.

Editor's Note: On sharing this story with Mrs. Hollowell before publication, she declared that any of Guilds' remembrances of her being anything less than perfect were most likely fiction.

Trucking Tomatoes

The islands south of Charleston, James and Johns Islands, empty into what is known as the ACE Basin. James Island, the island one passes through to get to Folly Beach, has been largely developed, while Johns Island is still the agricultural area of Charleston. Most of the produce that is sold at the Farmers Market around the city is grown on farms located on Johns Island. After passing through Johns Island, one passes over a small tidal Creek that separates Johns Island from both Kiawah and Seabrook Islands, the latter being made famous by the Nicholas Sparks movie The Notebook.

The last couple of years in high school, I would take 3 weeks in June during the tomato season and truck tomatoes on John's Island. The farmer I worked for was Clarence

Boyer. Clarence lived on River Road and was just a plain old country boy. He planted tomatoes on 3 or 4 different fields in the area. He had one way up in Hollywood, South Carolina. I used to hate going up there, especially at night because it was so dark, with no lights on the roads at all.

The way the day would usually go was you got out to the packing shed early around 6:30 or 7:00 a.m. and you would load up the truck with empty boxes to take out to the fields. My truck held 400 boxes and once they were full of tomatoes each would weigh about 40 pounds. Anyway, we would take the empty boxes to a field that Clarence would designate and then wait for the pickers to get out to the field. They would usually show up around 9:30 or 10:00. They had to wait for the dew to get off the plants before they would pick.

Clarence only used local pickers, he wouldn't use the migrant workers on the island. It seemed that locals were always coming from Summerville and they would show up in a school bus. The bus was supposed to hold 60 people maybe, but I know there would be 100 on the bus and that bus was rocking when they pulled up. Once they hit the fields and started to pick, it would only be a matter of minutes before we could start loading the truck with the boxes of tomatoes.

Once we were full we would take them to the packing shed. Usually there was a line so you wanted to get there as soon as you could to get close to the front. Once you off loaded your boxes, you had to get another 400 empty boxes and deliver them to another field and then start loading up full boxes again. We could almost always get 2 trips to the packing shed in one day and if you were lucky 3 loads but that was rare.

They started developing Seabrook Island around this time. Up until then it was just Camp Saint Christopher and some tomato and cucumber fields. Clarence grew some tomatoes on the island and so he would drive over there almost every day. When they started developing the island, they put a little 4x4 aluminum Pinkerton stand at the entrance to the island and you would have to stop and pick up a pass to be on the island.

Clarence would have nothing to do with that. There was no way in hell he was going to stop at a checkpoint when he had been coming over there all his life. There was no gate, so he would just drive right through. The guard would ask us to please talk to Clarence and ask him to get a pass so the guards wouldn't lose their jobs. But you know there was nothing we could do to change that.

One day, the guard actually stood out in the middle of the road and Clarence had to stop or run over the man. That made Clarence mad. One particular day, I was working with a fellow named Bruce who was from James Island. He was a big boy with long hair and a long beard, and sort of looked like Jesus. Bruce and I got back to Clarence's house around 11:30 after a long day and Clarence says, " Boys, I need your help with something."

We looked around and Clarence had loaded up the front end loader/backhoe on the flatbed and he said "Get in." We did as we were told and drove over to Seabrook Island. By this time the guard had gone home for the night. Clarence took that backhoe off the trailer and dug a huge hole. Then he turned around and picked up that little guard shack and dumped it in the hole. Clarence never had to stop to pick up a pass again. It ain't what ya know, but who ya know on those islands.

Big John is Shot

Charleston, being a port city, was a temporary respite for the sea-bound denizens who sailed the ocean for profit or punishment. East Bay Street, the closest street to the wharf, was the assembly point for tenements, watering holes and even a few houses of ill-repute that serviced this clientele. Squarely situated along these societal hinterlands in a blood-red building is Big John's Tavern, a virtual right of passage to manhood for many of Charleston's young men. Big John's is a throwback; an anachronism. While now East Bay Street is populated with world-class hotels and restaurants, stepping across the threshold transports the intrepid visitor back to the rough-and-tumble time where a glass bottle served double duty as both a beer holder and handy gavel with which to settle arguments.

When I was growing up you got your driver's license when you were fourteen, at least your driver's permit. I had mine and I would drive over the bridge to Charleston throughout my high school years to go to Big John's Tavern on East Bay street. Big John's was actually a membership-only club. I still have my membership card. Anyway the owner was Big John Cannady and he played nose tackle for the New York Giants back in the fifties...I don't know when exactly. He was a huge man and he always sat at the end of the bar.

His routine was to sit there from 5 o'clock till midnight when he closed, all the while drinking a case of Michelob. He would get up at 10:30 and go back to the bathroom. But that was the only time he would move. He had a side kick named Nooney Wilson and Nooney sat there next to John most of the night. Nooney was literally crazy and he would tell you the same joke every single time you walked into Big John's.

Anyway, every time I walked into Big John's, John would holler out, "Halloween, how you this evening?"

He knew you as you walked in the door.

I would always answer, "Great John!"

At the time, the drinking age was 18, and at Big John's this was often overlooked if Big John knew you. Furthermore, if you were black you could go into Big John's as long as he knew you or you were with somebody that he knew. So if any of my black friends wanted to come into Big John's, they were welcome as long as they were with me. It was a members-only club so John reserved the rights to serve beer to anybody he wanted to.

Right across the street was a plywood factory and the black workers across the way would come over and they would knock on the door. The door had one of these little diamond shape windows where you could see who was outside. John, from right where he sat, would lean back and push open the door and the guy would hold up one, two or three fingers, indicating how many beers he wanted.

John would say "Bobby, put a couple in the bag," or three in the bag or whatever and he never took any money. Given the prevailing rationale at that time, John did not “sell” a beer to a black man. At the same time, he was not going to deny anybody, especially a working man, a cold one after a shift. So Bobby would put two or three beers in a bag, hand it to them and that was that!

One night there is a knock on the door and John pushed open the door and this young fellow held up a small gun. He wanted John's money and he yelled "Give me all your money!"

Use your imagination as to what John said, but the gist was "If you want the money, go back there and get it, but I'll just stay here."

Now everybody was like "Hey, he ain’t getting off that stool." We were all scared; I am sure it took less than 60 seconds but it seemed like they argued for 10 minutes.

Finally, after what seemed like forever, the young fellow , beyond nervous, lost his cool and pulled the trigger. Big John was shot.

The way John was leaning back as he pushed open the door, his rather large belly was on full display. The boy shot him right through his blubber. John looked at that boy, jerked hard and grabbed him with his right hand. I don’t know if John was right or left handed but he grabbed him with his right hand and he pulled him into his left fist and knocked that boy out cold right on the ground.

This was about 11:30 when all this happened. John looked at Bobby and said "Bobby, lock it up at midnight. I am going to the hospital." He jumped into his white Cadillac Eldorado with the four little silver apples on the dashboard and went to the Roper hospital to get sewn up.

So there we were, trying to clean up the bar and get everything done, with the boy was still lying there out cold. After a while, the police came to arrest the boy and took him to jail.

The guy who was tending the bar, Bobby? Bobby was Bobby Hitt, now the Secretary of Commerce for the State of South Carolina. So anyway that's Big John's for you.

Future golf pro Guilds Hollowell
shows off his flawless form

Guilds and Caddie, the beginning...

CLIMB EVERY MOUNTAIN

Charleston has been known since it's founding as a place for religious freedom, with several religions actually being established here. Most notably is the Anglican Church, now know as the Episcopal Church, and colloquially known as "Catholic-Lite". Wherever there are four Episcopalians, there's always a Fifth...

This is more of a story about a man named Ben Hutto. Ben was a graduate of the Guad school and after he finished his post graduate work, he came back to what had now become Porter Gaud to become an English teacher. He also started the Fine Arts program at Porter Gaud and the Glee Club for high school students, as well as a small group known as The Chamber Singers.

I started with The Chamber Singers in its first year when I was in fourth grade and a boy soprano. The small group would travel a little but mostly we would sing around town and usually for many of the Episcopal high masses. If you think the Catholics have a high mass, you should see the Episcopal one. They were in Latin and more smoke and holy water than you could imagine.

One time, we were hired to sing at a local girl's wedding. It was to be a very solemn high mass service, most of it in Latin. We were dressed in these fancy robes with a very high frilly collar and the whole get up. The way the church was set up, the organ was behind us and we were facing across the sanctuary, so the congregation was to our left. With the organ behind us, behind a little alcove, Ben could not see the congregation directly but he had a system of mirrors where he could monitor what was going on. We followed him by looking into the mirror in front of us. It may not make sense to you but it worked.

The ceremony got underway and the bride came down the aisle to her future husband. She was wearing a gown that was very sheer up top and deeply cut and her cleavage was...impressive. She and her husband-to-be were facing the alter and we could see them out of the corner of our eye. She had her back to the congregation as the service progressed. The whole thing was in Latin and very formal. Only one problem...you just could not help but stare at her chest! To call it distracting was an understatement.

Ben was smiling because he could see from his mirror what was going on. So the service continued and after the vows were exchanged, things got funny. The bride turned to face her husband and from that angle the whole congregation could see her very busty profile. The best part was that just at that moment, her college roommate stood up and began singing Climb Every Mountain from *The Sound of Music*.

I don't know how we did not fall down laughing but we managed to control ourselves. Ben was laughing hysterically as he played the organ backing her up. He just might have wet his pants! Tears were running down his cheeks and he had a smile that was contagious. I really don't know how we kept it together until the end. I think I was in 9th grade but Ben's laughter that day is still a vivid memory for me.

Ben was a very talented musician. After leaving Porter Gaud, he took the job as the Dean of Music at the National Cathedral in Washington and I believed he played at Ronald Reagan's funeral. Ben died in 2016, but I did get a chance to sing one more time with him last year at a reunion of sorts of old Glee Club members at St. Luke chapel on the MUSC campus. Ben was remarkable. He could pull the best out of anybody and you wouldn't even know he was doing it until after it was over. He always made me feel so proud.

Disney World

Growing up in Charleston was not necessarily seen as special or exotic. What was really great was a family vacation to Daytona Beach or even to the center of a child's universe, Disney World. Five days and very long nights in a station wagon, salt water taffy and air-brushed t-shirts, it would take years to realize how special home was. Like the reporter who asked Charleston scion Amanda Rhett if she enjoyed traveling. Her reply? "Why should I travel; I'm already here."

I was on the phone with my daughter Ali the other day while she was in Disney World. She is a nanny in New York and her family was taking a few days vacation in Disney World in Orlando, Florida. Their dad had splurged and booked a private guide for the time they were there. That means all of the kids got to go right to the front of the line at each ride. Ali said they could ride 6 rides in less than 2 hours as opposed to 2 rides in 6 hours. She said to buy the pass was expensive. I told her the story of when the Glee Club went to Disney World.

It was in 1975 and Disney World was fairly new. The Glee Club was going to perform on one of the stages and we had rehearsed and had some time to kill before the actual show. We didn't think there was quite enough time to take any of the rides but then on our way off stage, a couple of us spotted some work coats hanging in the back. They each said "MAINTENANCE" on the front pocket.

So, what the hang, we put them on and started for Space Mountain. That ride was pretty new and the line was forever. We took a shot and went into the ride to the front of the line. The attendant just stopped everything and let us go check the ride for safety. It was pretty cool and so we figured, let's try the Country Bear Jamboree. It worked again! We didn't push it any further and we hung the coats back where we found them. Although a little nerve-racking, we didn't have to pay for that expensive private guide. I guess you have to take some chances just to know you're living!

Bingo

A church parishioner suggested Bingo as a way to raise funds for their church in financial troubles. However, after the priest invested in several sets of low-count Bingo cards, he learned that there were dozens of winners after each game. There was no way they could raise the funds to turn the church's financial woes around. The panicked priest contacted the inventor, Edwin S. Lowe, begging him to make the game more competitive. Lowe concluded that the cards needed more numbers – and in unique combinations. Working with a Columbia University math professor named Carl Leffler, Lowe's version had over 6,000 different variations of 5×5 cards. Leffler created each of those cards by hand – leading him to lose his sanity. (The only computers to do this job in 1933 were humans. Don't we have it lucky these days?)

I have not been kicked out of too many places, but it has happened occasionally.

The most embarrassing place was the big parlor on Sullivan's Island. Back in the early 70's there was a large pavilion on Sullivan's and every Thursday night all of the older people would get together and play bingo.

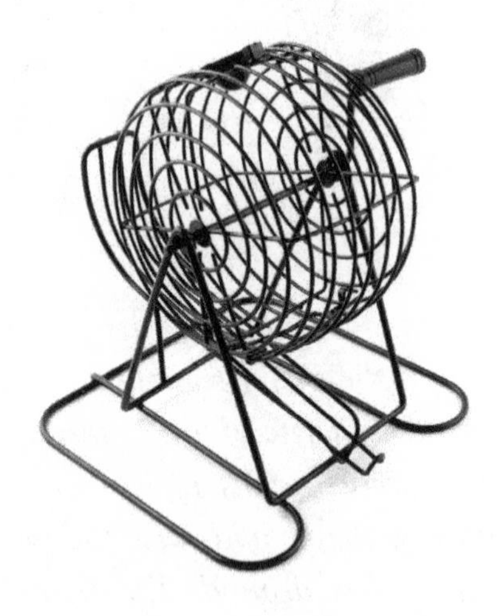

I had a friend named Larry and he was a couple of years older than me. One night we decided we would go visit the bingo game. I am sure we had a couple of beers before hand. Now this was before they played with a stamp and people used little chips to place on their number when it was called out.

Well Larry and I started the game and waited until there were enough numbers called out so that somebody might have bingo. We were playing also and so it was a little of a gamble to see how long you could wait but after plenty of numbers were called, Larry and I would holler "BINGO!" Everybody moaned and would dump their little buttons or chips off off the card and the guy would come over to check our card.

Of course we didn't have bingo and everybody was mad. We managed to do that one more time before they kicked us out and told us we were never allowed to come to the bingo hall again. I think I was maybe 15 years old and I thought, I can go to Big John's, but not the bingo hall. That seems odd!

Bus Drivers

The first school buses in Charleston were horse-drawn carriages known as "school hacks" or "kid hacks." They were being made by Wayne Works starting around 1886, though it's possible they were around even earlier. The first motorized buses were built on a Model T chassis, and appeared in the city in late 1920's. And like this story, I remember well a group of high school students taking a school bus on a school-sponsored camping trip, no adult chaperon provided...

The one constancy of my time in school was the school bus system. Granted, it might not be the first thing to cross one's mind, but it was always there, nonetheless. When I start thinking of some of the Glee Club outings and our mode of transportation, it was usually a school bus. Mr. Hutto would drive the bus but sometimes if he was going to meet us there for some reason, one of us would drive the bus. It was usually Brian.

Can you imagine sending a group of teenagers today on a school bus by themselves? Various "stuff" would be secreted onto the bus and the party would start. Jack and Jimmy playing "Sandman" in the back of the bus while a few would partake and enjoy the music. We got in trouble one time because someone decided that he would relieve himself outside the bus window while driving and the paint job on the bus did not take too kindly to that. I'm sure the passing cars were none-too-pleased, either.

I never took a bus because they didn't have one that came over the bridge to Mt. Pleasant: we were too far out. But as I recall, all of the buses that picked up the kids from in-town or West Ashley were driven by high school students. Like I said, I don't remember all of the details, but I'm pretty sure if you were 16 and had a clean record, you could be a bus driver.

I remember hearing stories of stopping off at McDonald's on the way home. Depending on who was on the bus, I think once the younger kids were dropped off, there might have been some detours taken on the way home!

Things have changed and probably for the better. Security needs to be higher because people seem to be getting crazier. I guess I sort of drove a bus as well... I had 4 younger brothers in the car with me so what is the difference?

Shark Fishing With Bruce

Shark, unlike today, was almost never utilized as a source of food for Charlestonians. Frankly, there were perceived to be tastier fish in the sea! But in one respect, Charleston was leading culinary progress. It wasn't until the 1950's that the rest of America began to appreciate shrimp, long a staple of Lowcountry fish-mongers, sold by the "swimpee" men on the peninsula.

I have mentioned Bruce before. He and I worked together sometimes trucking tomatoes. He was a James Island boy, big and strapping who looked like the pictures you see of Jesus; long hair and a big beard.

Bruce invited me to go shark fishing with him one Sunday. I was never big on the water (odd for a son of Charleston) but I did spend a little time on the water every once in awhile and shark fishing sounded like it would be fun. There was a shark hole right between Seabrook Island and Kiawah Island not very far off.

So I met him on Seabrook one Sunday and we put his little boat in. He had a 15 foot john boat with a little 15 horse Evinrude on it. We had a cooler in the middle of the boat full of beer and we headed off.

Now the shark hole was only about 200 yards offshore if that. It wasn't long before Bruce caught a shark. It was pretty easy to do and we were just catching sand sharks so nothing too dangerous. This one in particular though, was almost 5 feet long and Bruce managed to snag him and pulled him towards the boat. He used a gaff to hook the shark, wrestling him inside the boat. I almost freaked out.

You put two men, a cooler and a 5-foot shark in a 15-foot jon boat and that shark starts to look like Jaws. It got worse.

Bruce would use this little kitchen hammer to knock the shark out but it would take some doing. I would have chosen a large mallet but it wasn't my boat. I was sitting on the edge of that boat thinking to myself, "I don't want to be in this boat, but I don't want to be in that water either. "

Everything worked out fine. We took the shark around the corner to Rockville where there was this bait shop. They paid us 40 cents a pound for that shark and we didn't have to dress it or anything. I guess they cut it up for bait. That shark hole is still there today.

Water Tower

Affectionately referred to as "The Muni," The City Course opened in 1929 and has known a great deal of Charleston golf history. It has hosted the South Carolina State Championship and remains the home of the Charleston City Amateur. Incidentally, the first golf club in America was founded in Charleston in 1784.

I have done a bunch of stupid things in my life.

I remember once coming back into Mt. Pleasant in my friend John's station wagon. We were driving down the Highway 17 bypass, now Johnnie Dodds Blvd., and I decided to climb out of the back window of the car and crawl across the roof and back in the window on the other side. The funny thing is that I found out later that what the guys inside the car were really worried about was what they were going to say to my mother if something really bad happened, even though no one tried to stop me. Obviously nothing bad happened so I was lucky.

Another incident that sticks out in my mind happened just off of the Charleston Municipal Golf Course, the "Muni" as we all know it. I played a fair amount of golf with a fellow named Vance. Vance and I were a pretty good team and we would play some pretty serious money matches against grown men, lawyers and doctors and the like. For some reason they always thought they could pair up enough to take us, but more often than not they didn't.

Well this one time, Vance and I were headed down to Seabrook Island to play the brand new golf course that they had just built, the match was against two guys from Greenville in the Upstate. We stopped at the Muni to pick up a caddie. You could always find someone who would carry your bags at the Muni.

After the match, which we won, we stopped back by the Muni to drop off the caddie... and we thought we would have a little fun. We had done pretty well money-wise in the match so we figured we would goof off a little. It was fairly slow so we decided we were going to play the course backwards. We started at the #9 green and headed backwards towards the #9 tee box.

If you knew the course back then, when you are standing on the #9 tee box looking at the green, off to the right there was a water tower. Actually, the water tower was in a neighborhood that bordered the golf course, and is not there anymore. I am not sure why they took it down.

Well anyway, Vance decided it would be a great idea to climb the water tower and hit golf balls from the top. Sounded like fun to me so we dropped our clubs and took a hand full of golf balls and a 1 iron and started up the tower. When we got to the very top, there was a flat space about 6 or 7 feet across and if one person laid down, the other could hit a golf ball out toward Maybank Highway. There was a gas station on the highway that we could almost hit.

Well we didn't hit but a few balls before the James Island police were there. They hollered up with their bullhorn for us to stop and come down immediately. Vance looked down and hollered, "What are going to do with us? You can't arrest us!"

The policeman said he couldn't promise anything but we had to come down because it was not safe. Vance turned around and hit another ball out toward the highway.

I figured we were in jail for sure so what the hell. Vance hollered down again, "If you promise not to arrest us, we will come down."

He was also out of golf balls.

Well I don't remember the exact number of pleas that came from us, but we came down and by some miracle were not arrested. I think the officer was just happy that we didn't kill ourselves.

Vance could talk his way out of just about anything. He was a small fellow but had a huge presence. Unfortunately, Vance was killed in November of my senior year. A Sullivan's Island policeman was in silent pursuit with his lights off and t-boned Vance in his car right after Vance picked up his girlfriend. It was Vance's 16th birthday. We started a golf tournament in his name at Snee Farm. That tournament I believe has been renamed to the Junior Rice Planter's. Most Mount Pleasant folks from the 1970's would remember Vance.

Samuel Guilds Hollowell, Jr., in his signature hat, enjoying a cool beverage on Shem Creek.

CPSIA information can be obtained
at www.ICGtesting.com
Printed in the USA
BVHW082337161221
624066BV00003B/164

9 781927 458310